LIFE

ENCYCLOPEDIA

By

OKELOLA OLADAYO JOSEPH

Print by
goLEAN
in the Federal Republic of Nigeria

goleanbooks@gmail.com

www.booksbymagciwand.com.ng
+234-1-8418632, +234-8059864322

1, Bamisile Street Egbeda
Lagos, Nigeria.

DEDICATION

To man who walks and crawl on the soil,
Rising and falling just like the sun and moon,
Remember the creator
For there shall be sun after the rain,
Better days ahead
For all not to lose hope;
Victory continua.

ACKNOWLEDGEMENT

I die like a river when I forsake my source. All to you my creator, my life, creativity, strength, existence, my passion and the fountain of my understanding. To him who makes my life to be well, blessed be thy holy name. With a joyful heart, gracious smile, thunderous voice, clapping hands, moving legs, I say, thank you lord.

Much thanks to a friend, father, uncle, brother, adviser and my editor, **Brian Howland**. I appreciate your time and effort, and also your construction of wisdom and patience to see my book grow to an adult conclusion, I doff my hat for you sir.

So many years journey, growing to strand and hold a pen joyfully. Behind me was a woman – a mother, who stood and fought for me. I would have never discovered myself if she hadn't made me recover. To a human angel who caressed me with love and passion from when I was a boy to a man. All for you, **Mrs Adepeju Salami**

To the one who encourages me with heavenly words and prayers, always there for me just like a mother would res-pond to the cry of her child. I'm forever indebted to you sir, **Evangelist Olalekan Alfred (ACI)**

To my identical me but begotten before me, he who also carries the name my race bears, we both hold the paddle that sails through life. Thank you for being my compass and direction; your role as a brother has never been hidden, I love you, **Okelola Olajide Gabriel**

To my circle of motivators, they never sleep without a

word piercing my heart and reviving my zeal to keep writing. I call them confessors, confessing me to write till I'm taken and in love with words. Now I'm married to poetry.

To you, Funmilayo Williams, Olaonipekun Funmilola Racheal, Irekunle Ajeboriogbon Samuel, Olanrewaju Taoreed Abiodun Best, Olayemi Akewi, Prince Adekola Onafuwa, Mr. Adesanya Adetola, Samson Omayewa Ugbedeojo, Mr Sote, Mr Terwase Agaigbe, Agoro Samuel Olaoluwa, Goke Oyedokun, Promise Egwin,Adedoyin Harriet, Olawoyin Abiola Muheeden, Adeoti Tofunmi Adekunle, Segun Salau, Lisboa Olatoun Esther, Bunmi Adetoye, Oyebade Precious, Damilola Afolabi, Victor Oinu, Mosobalaje Gbenga, Olatunji Joseph Oladipupo, Pastor Joseph Keana, Pastor Wale Arowojolu, Freedom Kolade Olanrewaju, Glennie Joyce Williams, Ahniyah Smileymoore, Dominique, Ogbudu Ayobami Abigail (Oloori),Afolorunso Damilola,

FINALLY;
>   I stretch forth my hands
>   Holding you all to one
>   Like a chicken guiding it chicks
>   Slow words into your ears do i speak
>   This is just the beginning

Editors; *Brian Howland, Adedoyin Harriet, Rich Alzy*
Cover designer; *Osagie Sodiq Popoola*
Interior design; *Ehikhamen Samuel*
Reviewers; *Brian Howland, Iykee Edward, Vishnu Pandya*

CONTENTS

A PICTURE OF ME 15

A SONNET FOR LATE FR.ALBERT JUNGERS DEATH 17

AN INSCRIPTION OF AN UNKNOWN GOD 18

AN ORDAINED CALL 19

BE WISE 21

BEAUTY OF THE NATION 23

BOKO HARAM 24

BRING BACK OUR GIRLS 25

BROKEN HEART 27

CELEBRATION 29

CHANGE 30

CRYING PEOPLE 31

DREAM LAND 32

EARTH 33

FATE 35

FUTURE 37

GIVE IT A CHANCE 38

GRACE 40

GUILTY 41

HATRED LOVE 42

HEAVENS 43

HUMANS 44

IDENTICAL ME 46

INDEPENDENCE DAY 48

IT'S YOUR TIME 49

KILLERS OF MIND 50

LADIES OF DISPERIES...51

LETTER TO GOD..52

LIFE 53

MAKING IMPACT...54

MAMA'S SMILE 56

MISS YOU 57

MORTAL CLAIMS IMMORTALITY 58

MY RAP..62

NEVER LOSE HOPE..63

NOSTALGIA..65

ON MY WAY TO THE STREAM 67

PRAISE 68

SAFE JOURNEY 69

SAMSON OMAYEWA..71

SYMPATHY NEVER WORKS..72

TEARS WON'T DROP..73

THE CONFUSED LOVE MIND...75

THE JUST FIGHTER..76

THE LATTER RAIN 77

UNFORGETABLE DAY..79

NIGHT BATH...80

REVIEWS

My dear friend,

At this moment, your poetry is on my table, not on table only, but in my mind and heart too! Yes, I don't know you in detail. Not your today or background & you don't know me, but is it true? No. I don't think so. We are much closed travelers in the same boat! Our common medium is the world of the words! We are for, with and about words, the world of words. You said in a poem, "A picture of me" –where peace and love of all nature are inscribe/ it a home for all/the root and mother of my poems/ this is who I am.

Some more poem on love and pain also very touchy- ' A sonnet for late Fr. Albert loungers death', ' Boko Haram', 'Broken Heart' , 'Guilty', 'Hatred love', 'Ladies of Dispe', 'Miss you' are result of your mind and heart also!

I noticed that you are a poet of love, hope and suffering. Not individual but your concerned to the country and society. You said about 'Samson omayewe', 'never lose hope', 'Mortal claims immortality', 'Making impact', 'Killers of mind' and 'cosmic world' is your content.

There are many shades in these poems, from individual to eternal.

In your poem, we –reader –get more and more pain. What is this pain? Khalil Gibran - a well-known thinker poet- said, "Your pain is the breaking of the cell that encloses your understanding".

Yes we all are living with same wall- some desire. This pain and our world of the words creates poem! Once – Borice Pasternak – Nobel Prize winner post. From Russia- said: 'I want the heart of matter, the meaning, cause, foundations roots and kernels of vanished days.

Weldon, my friend.

You are a young voice of your country and society.

Congrats!

Vishnu Pandya (Gujarat, India)
Author of 98 books on history Professor in journalism

We know of stories that touch the heart, in this collection, Dayo pens poetry that touches the soul.

The first poem in this collection of brilliant words reveals the identity of the young voice rising as the cool sea breeze. His poetry is refreshing and revealing.

Who is this? What is this?

Life Encyclopedia is an amazing collection of poems and spoken words. In the opening piece the poet in, 'a picture of me' says in moving words...my heart is all I got/ bearing the mind and pain of others/ so fragile and loving/where peace and love of all nature are inscribe/ it a home for all/the root and mother of my poems/ this is who I am.

The truth indeed. Dayo does bear the mind and pain of others and in his own words- pure, creative and delightful to read, he expresses emotions that only the skillful hand of a crafted poet can. Or as he puts it so aptly in one of his titles: still marries a pen. Dayo has married a pen the offspring of the union is this beautiful bouncing book. life Encyclopedia however is not just about others and the shared burden of pain. In some titles the poet expresses death, the destructive memories of boko haram, and the voice of wailing like Rachel weeping for her children, but they are no more. in the piece titled 'bring back our girls'...won't we hear their voice?/will they silence their noise?/will they see the light? It is a great work and it painfully brings to mind the agony and sorrow of a nation, waiting, hoping and mourning... death hits her skull by a stone/I know her spirit will call/ will there be a remedy to run?never!/ they won't even have a tomb.

This work will inspire people to dream, have hope, think of the future and aspire change and faith.

The poet shows his class in the piece ' mortal claims immortality', the unique blend of Yoruba and Igbo with English is a worthy read. ' his rap' another entry, makes your head nod in quick beats.

The work is a broad collection of pieces. There are two or three collaborations between the poet and others; he also shares a few personal encounters... a personal loss, love, life triumph. Dayo's personal testimony is clear in his works.

Dayo is not just a poet. He is a prophet. His words heralding the 'latter rain'. He has poured out his vision and dreams in this wonderful collection of poetry that speaks and reaches out to your soul.

It is an amazing book. Indeed. Let the rain fall.

Iyke Edward Dike (Nigeria)
An author, writer, creative director and an editor
Author of the book Hearts asylum

I just finished reading your new book Life Encyclopedia!

"This is who I am" I am very pleased with it. "Bring Back Our Girls" expresses the struggle and trying to understand the EVIL that is Boko Haram.

"Be Wise", I must quote you:

"I long for thy wisdom for I am captured by thy love". This was like an arrow of love straight to my heart. It expresses how I feel about God too I recommend this book to everyone. It is a sincere poetic gift from you to everyone who cares about their fellow man, and ladies too!

Brian Howland
Public Speaker
(Toronto, Ontario USA)

PREFACE

The word encyclopedia was borrowed from a book called encyclopedia, where detailed information on varieties of subject are gotten.

Life encyclopedia focuses on every aspect of man's existence – struggles, religion, politics, race, human nature, natural resources and so many other varieties of information about life's encounter. All buttresses on giving hope and a better tomorrow.

This collection of poems speaks to the living, giving memories of experience, showing life solutions, and leading a good path for generations to come.

Life thou art thee
You make man hope for the best
Without thee there shall be no earth
What a grace bestowed upon thee
I pray i found your rest
All in one peace

LIFE

ENCYCLOPEDIA

A PICTURE OF ME

Who is this?
Thinking like none to say
The silence of a poet
Says more beyond just words
Just like the elders
Who breathe in and exhale out
Cause words of wisdom has bounced in

More in him
That life could bring
Powerful, strong, piercing like two edged sword
Beyond coal and fire
Eyes with an ex-ray vision
Lips filled with smile
Begat words of life
Edifying the minds of men
Hands, never shaken or wrinkled
Still marries a pen
That births a flow like a river
Ears
Sensitive to the breeze of words
So inspired with the lyrics of the day
His nose sucking the breathe of life
To live and write
Like the breathe bestowed on Adam
My heart is all have got

Bearing the mind and pains of others
So fragile and loving
Where peace and love of all nature are inscribe
It a home for all
The root and mother of my poems
This is who I am

A SONNET FOR LATE FR.ALBERT JUNGERS DEATH

Eyes haven't shown to me who thou art
But grief was all it could bring
I got to know of your impact
Your ink that liberate all being

Death has been unfair
Taking the one who is our friend
Giving us nothing but tears and fear
Far from us but not till the end

All in all you have amend
Legacy that no one could compare
Father and child we could blend
Your presence is what we see in the air

I'm hopeful
For thy words has made our minds full

AN INSCRIPTION OF AN UNKNOWN GOD

Eternal creator of mankind
Beginning of reigns and unending existence
Giver of life and death
Worthy are you among gods
Lover of nature and human soul
First of all truth
Immortal kings
Ageless being
The only wise one
Mighty are your wondrous works
In your presence is
Your awesome majesty
Of your kingdom
Is of no end

AN ORDAINED CALL

There are many calls we could hear
Many flaws we could bear
Though time seems not to be near
But I know we all will be there

A spirit so strong that would speak
Fighting all battles life could adopt
Can't be hindered never be tampered
Curse could wage in one force
Just a try to hold the day
An impossibility event to the world to come
It springs forth like the day
Shining even to all who couldn't see
Destiny calls waking the dose
Standing for those who couldn't breathe
A call of hope about the future disclosed
Bringing courage to those that are chained
We all awaits your time to show

Where do I belong?
The heating of a fleeting thorns drum
Past archive a windy storm
Enclosed my heart all in pain
Never rest like a hare racing for fame
Darken routes where memory less gain
Bare foot on thorns oh slave saw
Oh destiny an ordained call

Slow the forest beetle whistle call
Men's past struggling, heaven sing rain
Now new name tagged high all gain
Courage gazed yesterday for latter aim
Trying pace diverting slowly down
Singing sweet song of memory before dawn
Hold strong when it pains as difficulties strike
All black turns white as thy courage strike

This is collaboration between ME and VICTOR OINU

BE WISE

I choose knowledge
To behold the truth
I embrace understanding
For my heart is full of merriment for thy peace
I long for thy wisdom
For I am captured by thy love
To know thy right and thy wrong

I slow to speak
For my inner mind needs edifying
I listen to thy word
That I may gain wisdom

Knock, knock, knock, on my door
Who art thou?
I am thou; wisdom
For my fear is plentiful in thy house

Heaven is all I need
Proverb voiced:
Thou son, turn thy ears to wisdom
Apply thy heart to understanding
I give wisdom
And my mouth is full of knowledge and understanding

Stick with me
And thou shall be blameless
I will save thee from the wicked

Never forget me, never
And thou shall be wise

BEAUTY OF THE NATION

Hail to thee, O ye Nasarawa
You are thy womb of thy state
The life of the people
How great thou are
Thou home of solid minerals

KEANA, thou pace setter
Whom calls all to bow
You are the existence of thy state
Thy taste is unquenchable
You are the uniqueness of the nation
Thy strength of the ancient is within
You rise like the sun
Your shining light leads the part for others
How priceless you are
Home of ancient salt

TOURISM; as fragile as life
Calm as gel
Beauty of the nation
Thy passion is not challenging
You are far beyond eagles
Unstoppable strength you have got
You are treasures that can't be cast away

BOKO HARAM

Sting like a bee
Cling to the heart of man
I heard of vampires
Thought all are in extinct
Now you bring memories
Memories of how destructive they become
Your passion is beyond that
All you thirst for
Was flesh and blood
Would that be thy survival? Never....

I know of haram
Abomination is what it speaks
Has the beast in thee not committed that?
Blood splits like the rain fall
Fall and flows like a mighty oceans
Ocean echoes beyond whirlwind
How thick blood is before water
In time and season all will voiced
Voiced like thriller
Piercing you one after the other
Like a two edged sword
Till thou fall asunder
And nothing will be your cover
Boko haram

BRING BACK OUR GIRLS

Won't we hear their voice?
Will they silence their noise?
Will they see the light?
Will all once again be bright?

Theirs is a flow in my eyes
Flow beyond the deep blue sea
Consumed with pains and sorrow
Heart filled with burdens no one could lift
When I see the innocent been punished
This is unbearable
I can't take it no more
Men's death beyond animals
Will the bloodshed be a remedy for the land?
No, no, no, no
Let my eyes and ears live in doubt
Lives not valuable
All stoned to death like the disciples
Is this a judgment upon the nation?
Is end time truly near?
Lips shivering and heart bleeding
No I don't want to cry
Bleeding in captivity of our loved ones
She showed me to be brave
Death hits her skull by a stone
I know her spirit will call
Will there be remedy to run?
Never!

They won't even have a tomb.

BROKEN HEART

A wounded heart
Hurt feelings
All renders tears in my eyes
Wish I could turn hands of time
Heal the scars and wound
Cure the pains and grief
Desired I haven't caused any hurts
But was wrapped up with days of youth
Feeling been un top
Filled with pleasures of strength and love
Pains and sorrows in memories have I brought
Hunting me till eternity
My hurts changed their focus
Bought them nightmares
Never was I remorseful
Now it all bounced at me
Insincere feelings and pains I sow
Reaping it harvest I see
Love shared with me but blind to see
My wickedness and selfishness showed to me
Love I need couldn't get
My act has chased away the right one
All left alone
They shared all they had
Devilish was I leaving them naked
In pretense covered with leaves called marriage
For time pass waiting for my cover
I was far away couldn't be found

Now I could see their broken hearts
Bouncing on me often

CELEBRATION

Merriment is the day called
For the existence of a new born king
Whose call was to liberate all mankind
Men jubilate for that great day
Smile fills all heart
Bringing all to a new life, a new beginning and a new hope
Merry Christmas and happy New Year

A year of the genesis of man
New beginning new creation
Aspirations are new
Desires are renewed
Thirst and hunger erupt
Ignited for the attainment of success

Now is the rising of the sun
Where lace are been buckled
Take the chance, before the setting of the sun
It's a start for the brave
Give doors to wisdom
And thou shall have great success
Merry Christmas and happy New Year

CHANGE

I need a new life
A life been freed
Free from all hypocrisy
A life of the real me

Life of my own
Governed by my conscience
Standing to be upright
Choosing what is blessed

Never to please others
Never desirable to the heart of others
Death befalls the identical me
Stepping my feet to the real me

I stand firm with my shoulders high
Gazing up with an eagles eyes
Sticking to truth and despised injustice
A change is all I need

CRYING PEOPLE

I know how they felt
Their pains like the sands in the seas
I want to feel it touch
To know how life has been a grace for me.

A crying world
A world that chooses its own people
Heart weeps every moment
Hopes like gnashing of teeth
It is like a wait;
For the manifestation of a Messiah
To be delivered from chains and bondage.

I will always remember
My life isn't mine
Never will it be
They all need the smile again
Clothed with robes
Like the palace of David
Their suns have been hidden
Let grace cause sunshine
And we stand again like Cherubim.

DREAM LAND

I have a dream
To be great
Standing for the truth
Injustice will I ever fight

I choose the path of righteousness
Showing the way like the disciples
My thunderous words
Liberating people from the captivity of wilderness

I take my step at a time
Never will I lose my way
Though the troubles may be tough
Forever will I be there.

EARTH

A land called planet
Never Pluto, Saturn nor mercury
I know of one called earth
Unknown world for all
Like a living field
All striving for daily bread was it promised
Wrapped up with gifts of pains and gains
Sorrows and joy never ending
Battles here and there
It's a survival of the fastest
Earth, a beautiful garden
Gardens of aliens
Aliens of two, three, four feet
All still dwells in six feet
What gain are thou in thy beauty
Beauty that call man to vanity
Do thy grace speaks everlasting
I live to see thy purity
You condemn the mighty
At last the living ends with nothing

Oh mother of man
Beauty and kindness of all thine
Home to all, forsaken none
Bringing warmth and cold for all to embrace
Thy seeds have sprang
Thy multitudes untold
But now they have forgotten you

Stripping you bare
They have chopped thy trees and lard thee black
They have stained thy grounds now barren at thou
They have defiled thee and offered thee blood
Ooh earth thy beauty fades
But rekindled thou be
Let's take a stand to make all green
Let's redeem this land and make it a whole

This is a collaboration poem by ME and MUGANA DUNAMIS

FATE

Have got one life to live
Wouldn't let that happen in my dream
Longed for many years now at the brim
When Adam meets his Eve

I aspire and wish to explore
Beyond this I am now
My search and hopes hasn't ended for many years
Wish I could hear an angel voice
Showing me a path to take
For I know the future is now

I climbed the mountains and hills
Looking for the right one to lead me through
Hungry to know the voice within me
That speaks of you about the future
When all my worries would be filled with answers

We walk in different land of unknown
In a battle field day after day
A pen, ink and a book
Like a sword, shield and armor
Putting them in writings
Like killing all enemies within
Legend and tales has been spoken
About the meets of two warriors
Speaking out lyrical words like poison
Now we stand just two facing

All wasn't for violence
It a prophecy coming to past
But fate draws it near

FUTURE

Where will I be?
Words I can't answer
Heart troubled daily
Scared what the future has for me
Will I make it?
It's the word speaking inside
Lord! I am scared
I don't wanna be in doom
Fear grips the heart of man
Worried of the unseen
Flesh doesn't want the pains
Free like the birds in the sky we all want
Shining like the day
Powers to decide the future
Lies in the hand of the creator
We give the best
Establishment comes from the supreme
Ordaining from the heavens
I would rather stick to my source
Pleaded before the throne of mercy
And I would smile
Fearless from all unseen
And my ways will be prosperous

GIVE IT A CHANCE

Your eyes are my mantle
Staring at it leaves me bold
You rule my world
You rule my all

Your hug reminds me of a newborn child
Consumed with the passion of a mother
You changed the whole in me
And brought me to the kingdom of manhood

Why hate men?
Why taking what makes me a man
Thy merriment of your heart is my strength
I desire not your hatred bestowed on me
Forgive man forgive me

You have been hurt with promises been betrayed
Love not reciprocated
Trust been failed
Emotions been killed
That isn't all life has in store

There are lights after darkness
Sun after rain
Joy after pain
You just have to let go of the past

Am in love with you EBI

I love you like I want my life
At thy distance your love becomes stronger
A new beginning is all I want with you
You are my breath
Please make me breath

I believe in you
Let me share the pains with you
My bed is dead without you
Let me hold thy hands
In the ears of crowd
Echoes the words I do, I do, I do
Overwhelmed by you
Please give it a chance

GRACE

Death would have been my possession
Knocking at the door like a call
Insanity was always beside me
Taking me to an unknown world
Never had the power to resist
All because of you
Always mindful of me

Thousands of times wrong was I always
At the tick of the clock
Ever worthy was I not
Thy commandment I have never perfected
A life full of danger was I living
But you still preserve my days

Grace
Thy love and mercy
Can't comprehend what it looks like
Thy power works in me uncontrollable
Never deserves it
Strong always on me
Favor unmerited it brings my way

GUILTY

Felt lonely and confused
Felt guilty that I wasn't treating you well
Felt an emptiness within me
Cause your absence beats me every moment
At every bit of my heart
My conscience hunts me
Like have disobeyed the laws of nature
It hits me deep
That at my happiness, I became sad
Thinking I have never put a smile to your face
From the north, south, east to the west
The wind blows over me
Bringing your thoughts and memories
They whisper to my ears
Telling me how much you cared for me
Then tears again dropped from my heart
Now I know I have betrayed your emotions
Now I know you deserve more than the best
Do I still deserve your forgiveness?
To live a life of a changed person
I wanna put a smile to your face again
Please forgive me`

HATRED LOVE

I would forever despise you
Pains was all you brought me
Through the sun and the moon
My heart was never fed with peace
Because of thy non reciprocal love

Thought you are the treasure looking for
The integrity was never found
At the tip of your fingers
You could get all
Never will you be a woman of virtue

Hypocrisy, heartless, devilish, that's you
Thy womb is cursed
Thou unfaithful woman
Woe unto thy off springs
Shame befalls them all
You deserve not to live
I know God will forgive

HEAVENS

I live by thy word lord
To be equipped by thy spirit
Your lead is my desire
Guiding me till the end of time

Heavens
An angel wings gloriously shown
The majesty throne and honors
Heads bow down with thunderous worship

It's my place I want to be there
My baritone voice; singing hosanna
My eternal home at last
Never will it pass me by

He sits
Putting his eyes on me
Till I come
To be with you lord

HUMANS

The imperfect people
Backsliders
Their words are always been void
Words never defended
They chastised with words at your back
Never get the courage to speak at thy presence
Shameless they will ever be

Thy pit is been dung, if thou go at their words
They speak like the Pharisees and Sadducees
Showing they know all
Pretending knowledge is at their footstool
Their voice are heard at the court house
Disguising they are there for you

Never hearken to their words
For they are like the cunning devil
Whose presence is filled with destructions
Lips filled with promises unfulfilled
Hearts like the venom of a viper
Filled with the well of corruption
Truth do they despise
They eschew change
In pains and sorrows will they ever live

They are not the best friend to rely on
They lead the way to danger
Vanished like the dust in the air

Leaving you naked to the evil life has

They enticed with words like the forbidden fruit
Killing the morality's in you
Till thou look worthless and unworthy
And thy words has no life again

IDENTICAL ME

Satisfying you is all I have ever done
Never want to see you cry
Passionate, laying my life for you
But wrongs were what you did to me

My actions are right to you
Pure in hearts were my intentions
Giving all, nothing hidden
For you to be happy and get satisfied

A reciprocal heart was all I wanted
Taking my pains and I sharing yours
Washing you with hyssops night and day
For thy shame to be hidden
Desired never to let you feel pain
But thou scratch my back with thorns

Selfishness was thy watchword
A beast in a sheep cloth is who you are
Pretended you are there and would be there
Never knew you are far away all times
I thought thy passion of love would reciprocate

Am living in thy battle all day long
Neglecting mine, pursuing yours at all time
Willing to see the smile in your face every moment
I cared for you
A life not mine am living in

For thy sake only
Heartless you are
This isn't the real me
It's the identical me
Tracing back my steps is all I will do
Feeling the pains for you no more

INDEPENDENCE DAY

O hail, to freedom
Casting out from thee, bondage
You hold my strength in chains
Like mortals am I all day long

Nights and day am all blind
To behold the treasures you have got
Thy scepter is hidden
When will I rule again?

Shining like the sun, do my spirit longs for
My glory is like the day
Can't be touched, never will you be harmed
Cause thy presence is thy mantle
You will forever rise
O Independence Day

IT'S YOUR TIME

You are the best
You settle for no less
It's yours
It's your world
You are created for such a time as this

Fight for the best
You can't be traded for
You forever are a priceless being
Your smiles set the pace
Am proud of you
My head keeps nodding

The end justifies the means
You have got a moving spirit
Don't be discouraged
Very much the stumbling blocks could be
Theirs a prevailing gift in you
Time to unleash the potentials within
Have confident
And just believe

KILLERS OF MIND

Hypocrisy, gossips
They all lose
Lonely they all become
Instability falls upon them

Ants they are
They pick at you in the back
Their teeth are visible at thy presence
Showing all like a saint
Homeless will they be at the end

They eschew wonders
They are the forbidden fruit
Never to have encounter with
Canniness is their ways
Forever will they lose
And smile will be a curse

LADIES OF DISPERIES

All in differences
Coming to the place of his sanctuary
All in colors of dresses
Faces painted of a clown

I watch them with wonders of heels
Dancing and dragging through like Fulani cows
Ticking of the clock they move step by step
Saying they have come to worship and praise

Heads bow down to worship
At the majesty presence
Tell me who can point finger at a king
No one, no way
Cause death awaits and never be feigned

Let all come with a dancing shoes
Singing and merry in his presence
Far beyond David in his palace
Signs and wonders does it provokes
Till satisfaction befalls the heart

Been cloth but still naked
They murmured it's the latest
But in his kingdom outdated
Never rated as been daughters
All he could see was an outcast

LETTER TO GOD

You will forever be my lord
My life and moments are gripped in thy hands
Never will I go astray
Always will thou draw me near

I have the stubborn nature within
You feigned my flaws
Thy love is too unconditional
Your mercy is like the breeze

I despise my wrongs
To be free from iniquity
Welcome back, is all I do again
I don't wanna live like this no more

Thou everlasting shepherd
Who pampers and comfort me
I need you more today lord
Thanks for thy mercy and grace

LIFE

Life, how unfair art thou
Thy ruling powers can't be controlled
You bestow grace upon who you pleased
Far beyond been spelled

Thy kingdom is in thy world of man
Your command is from no one
Pains and gains are enriched in your throne
Foolish confront the wise at your decree
How mysterious in the hearth of man you are

You are the Achilles of man
Never challenged by the living
A curse can't be unveiled in human's planet
I am powerless at thy presence
Thy mercy will I forever seek

MAKING IMPACT

Why art thou self
Why is thy footprint, I, Me, mine, myself
Life isn't all "alone"
He who lets go of his life has it

I chose to make impact
Troubled to know my call
Dismayed to please God
What does He expect from me

Then my heart goes back to thy word
If thou loveth me feed my lamb
How do I love you?
He says: love thy brother
Do I have love?
He answers; I give freely because my love is unending

A call from above
Feed my sheep
My heart pursed
Who are his sheep?
He opens my eyes to the 24th of Deuteronomy

Am confused Lord
This is my unquenchable thirst
How do I feed thy sheep and thy lamb?
12th and 13th Corinthians roared
Love!

Love is patience and love never fails
It's the greatest of all
This is your ministry
Now I found my purpose

MAMA'S SMILE

Joy at last blasted out from her heart
Men thought she can't be heard
God then showed his ways first
Now sorrows and pains has reached it end

Tears and cries no more
Seeing the smiles down her lips

Praising for no more closing door
And end to the curse of many years

Breaking down will she ever be
Illnesses will she long lived
If you ever leave
No air will she ever ever breathe

Let her smiles see no end
Forever called blessed

MISS YOU

Life sails like a ship
It brings it end back to the shore
Love restores back what was lost
It draws back the heart of the brave
Romeo will always find his Juliet
Though I could travel thousand miles
When love opens the key to your heart
I will be back and near
When am been bonded by your love
The beauty in your smiles
Brings me home to you
Cause I can never live without seeing your smiles
Your looks and eyes
Speaks to me
It says how tenderly you are
Calmness is in your eye
I found peace in your looks
Fun to be with
A day without your presence
It like life been taking away
I miss you and I missed your echoes

MORTAL CLAIMS IMMORTALITY

Nature, life, creation
All brings human to earth
Time begins it counts on men
They seems to be like gods
Perfect in all their ways
They hold the power to be a judge
All like the Pharisees and Sadducees
Never knew they have got a stain on their garments
Life brought men to be one
One all in love peace and unity
But all they could share was woe
They call for everlasting and one mind
All that seems to last was evil
I still recall the words of fire that proclaims
"He without sin should be the first to cast a stone"
Hath thy stain not been reviewed?
No one was ever worthy of justification
Wrongs judged wrongs
Do we then have the future called everlasting?
When our heart is creating a doom
Theirs could only be a life of immortality
When all wrongs are right
When love isn't scarce
When peace is reviewed
And when those that falls are lifted by others

Aye ko lo bi opa ibon
Eda adarihurun n sebi oba oke

Ti n gbaye pase
Ko seni to le lo ile aye gbo
Eniyan a gbowo l'ohun gbogbo bi oba aye
Aisodo omo eniyan ni n mu aye dorikodo
Ole n mu ole
Elese n dajo elese
Eniyan agbeyin bebo je
Olufokantan ti a ni ko feniloju
Igba ata lo fi senu
Nje iwo adajo ti n dajo
Ti yo ipin oju re bi?
Aye a fi omo eniyan sowo
Eda a f'emi sofo
Aso funfun ni iru won n mu rode
Won sora won di olowolayemo oniwa rere
E je ki a n'iwa tutu,ti n yo obi lapo
E je a se aye ni iwotun wosi
Aye a toro,a dun gbe.

Nature to thy nature
Double, double toiled and trouble
All over thy nature
Mortality claims to be immortal
Blames full thy mouth
Evil and wickedness cover thy souls
Oh! Aye! , thou are nothing but earth soil
Please deceive not the nature again
Now I realize we are nothing but mortals not immortal
You Mr. know all
You Mr Novice who true and throw yourself to thy

wallet
To get false alarm because your brain has tied with
corruptions and negatives
With the help of thy peanuts in your mouths telling thee
That men are immortal
You then turn your response to amen
Given to ye prophet of doom
Covered with alarmist
Woe again to ye who claims to be immortal

Ihe ojoo na arizi ibe ya elu
Nji isi oche ewere obara mere mmiri on'un'u
Ma chefuo na obu obara mmadu ibe ha
Ndi ojoo jizi abali mere ehihie
Ha ekweghizi na mmadu na anwu anwu
Ma na oburu na ihe ojoo gba afo amara
onye mere ya

Master of immortality
You have used your powers to destroy our hut
And then use your authority to lay our peace to ambush
But never to forget
That all nature is to soil
And soil is to nature
Meanwhile, over bed have decorated to six feet
For every nature to witness when your mouth shall kiss
the soil of the earth
Be you boss or servant
We are nor immortal but mortals
Please to nature again

The beds are of the same aesthetic beauty of the same measurement

This is a collaboration between ME and NWOBODO SOLOMON, which we also added our dialects both in Yoruba language and Igbo language.

MY RAP

I wonder and ponder
God is a wonder
Jesus is my father
And I don't need a mother

Life isn't a danger
Jehovah is my keeper
Have got a hammer
Who is Jehovah shammah

I go faster
With Jesus as my driver
I can't die in a river
Cause the spirit taught me as a swimmer

I laugh with wonders
My walls have been under
Though am in the summer
Jah is still my warmer

NEVER LOSE HOPE

It seems your prayers aren't answered
Never lose hope
It seems your labors are in vain
Never lose hope
It seems all your fasting and supplications are
starvations
Never lose hope
It seems you are the only one earth isn't pleased with
Never lose hope
It seems enough is enough
Never lose hope
It seems all the good deeds isn't harvesting
Never lose hope
It seems the day of merriment isn't near
Never lose hope
It seems all isn't in favor of you
Never lose hope
It seems it the end of the world
Never lose hope
It seems change isn't coming
Never lose hope
It seems death is calling
Never lose hope
It seems the sun won't shine and the moon won't stand
Never lose hope
It seems the land would never be green

Never lose hope
The harvest is near
Never lose hope
Be patient
Never lose hope
Cause life is all about time

NOSTALGIA

My feelings like been home again
Feelings arouse like joy within
I love this home
Wish it never ends and, forever be

Smiles fill this face
Lips filled with melody and words of old
Though twenty kids can't play for twenty years
We all meet again with news of the journey
Journey of life and battles been won

Strength is built in the youth
The old become weary
Feels home again
Seeing the image of the past
Of all the victories won
My strength is restore back
Never will I fear the future
The unseen will never consume

Time again, we depart
Like the sail of a ship
I speak farewell with a waving hand
Don't wanna see you go again
I won't drop the waters from my eyes
Farewell again
Facing the battles of life
We will meet again know

With victories
For we will conquer

ON MY WAY TO THE STREAM

I think I saw an angel walking down the stream
Can't get my sight off her
So beautiful to behold
She makes me feel good
What a blessed day
A good Monday in my white attire

You captured my mind
Your thoughts are all around me
Never will I let you go this time
Never

The whitening of thy teeth just like the beginning of the
day
That gives light to all creatures
To a wonderland would thy lips be
When pressed with mine

Thy fairness leaves no spots like the road to paradise
Are you human, I ask myself?
Thy creation is too perfect
Strongmen will forever fall at thy feet
Because of your smiles and the space in your teeth
Are too powerful to gaze at
I call you a human angel
Molded from the hand of a supreme being
Called the perfectionist

PRAISE

Giving thanks to whom?
To him maker of life
Morning may fall like night
His changing still becomes unchanging
Forever remains the same
Let the lord be praise

Hard time may fall
Bad time might never cease
Tears could fall like rain
Mercies forever endures
Never let thy praise be stopped

Death could fall again
Sorrows could rise the same
Evil befalls them they would say
Change is what they would pray
Praise is what they would pay

Broken heart still remains the same
Trust broken and denial
Loved ones swept away
All we need is change
Praise greatly cause a change
Lord forever should be praise

SAFE JOURNEY

Safe journey
To the land unknown
A journey of a new beginning
In the midst of alien

A new world worth living in
A journey of a race
Race like a battle
That leaves a crown at the end

Go, go, go
Take a step at a time
Give romance to patience
It takes time
Perseverance should be thy shield
Be slow and steady

Have faith
Slow to rush
What you don't have he believes you are in need not
All takes time and season
All will be well someday
Thoughts and desires will surely come to pass
Patience Habakkuk 2:3-3

Happy am I for this day
Dreams are been accomplished
Race of life is triggered

It's a journey alone

Make thy faith strong
In tribulations and trials
Cling to him more and more
Like never before must thou cling
He holds thy path
Till we meet again
And we smile

SAMSON OMAYEWA

My friend and my brother
Emptiness of the heart is all without you
You deserve a throne in my kingdom
My heart is my kingdom
I give it all

Thy satisfaction is beyond drunkenness
Your impacts changes the whole me
Thy presence makes me rule
Am bold when you stand by me
Always will my heart cherish you

My debt to you all like the sun and moon
Forever will they shine till the end of the world
Your sincerity feigns all curses
I love you
Glad I found you
Samson Omayewa

SYMPATHY NEVER WORKS

I cry, I wept
All they long
Thinking life would change
Thinking life would behold sympathy on me
All was vanity begotten vanity

My heart ponders
My knees are bent
Am sheltered with sack cloths
Thinking life would bless me with mercy
But all was vanity begotten vanity

I found out life remains constant
Life has no life
Life is dead without you
You are life
Life is you
Cause life is what you want it to be

Life would never be shaken
Take the battle in your hands
Fight it
Win it
And rule it
Then life breaths again.

TEARS WON'T DROP

I see pains, sorrows
I see a golden spoon turns to clay
Greenish trees now brownish
A royalty feeding a pauper
All brings shame and mockery
But my tears won't drop

My eyes are swollen
Filled with an ocean of waters
Shining like the early sun
It glitters beyond gold
From all the worries life has got
For earth turns it back ears to my voice
Like blessings and favor been sealed
Heart cries like engine of a train
For destiny to reign
Still tears won't drop

It my stage of humility
To see what life has in store
Feeling the taste of the poor
It a lesson for the palace
When thy scepter is in thy hands
To love and to cherish
Be merciful and compassionate
Killing the seed of greedy
A shepherd over his sheep
My tears won't drop

Cause I won't.

THE CONFUSED LOVE MIND

You won my sight
Thy words tears my heart apart
I am melted like a wax
Who art thou?
Who took my breath away

I am been confessed by thy presence
You are possessed by an imaginary power
Your thoughts can't be feigned
Am incomplete like a new child

Where is me?
My ego has been left astray
I choose not this, cause I wanna be me
I don't want love no more
But at the sounds of your name
I keep doing what I desire not

Can 'comprehend you not
You changes like the day
Am like a clown in thy presence
Insatiable is who you are
Am imperfect in thy sight
Vanished by the man in me
Weak like the dust
I want to let go
But don't want to lose you

THE JUST FIGHTER

They call me honorable
Wonder if I am truly able
I have a God who is able
Incredible, unspeakable, adorable
My desires are unidentifiable
I can't be stopped or moveable
Echoes of my speech are audible
Their worries are imaginable
On my shoulders their pains are carryable
Sorrow befalls and made them disable
I will fight for you
For them, it will be unbearable

THE LATTER RAIN

How I wish
Like the words of the prophet saying
The latter shall be greater than the former
Zealous where they all
His presence strong and powerful all through
Signs and wonders never cease
All was for his glory

With the voice of him
Spoken through Joel
My spirit been poured out on the last day
Sons and daughters all shall prophesy
The young and thy old
Visions and dreams will they see
Wonders and signs thou seeth in heavens and earth
below
Let there be a fall again
Shower us with thy rain again
Harlots now in church today
All born to human activities
For the pleasure of the flesh
Back to our first love should we go
Love and passions unending
All stains swept away
Like the market in his sanctuary
Worship and praise day by day

His words never be little
Making it sharper than a two edged sword
Piercing all asunder
Not for self
But serving everlasting lord forever
And there shall be his glory, honor and power
Forever more
Amen

UNFORGETABLE DAY

Victory at last
These have I ever longed for
To walk and never to stumble
To the peak of success

Dreaming all night long
To be clothed in AJUWAYA
Serving my country at the clarion call
Forever my heart will be filled with gratitude

NIGHT BATH

I saw a cat
When I went to the bath
It was in the night
All was a blackout
Blood rush through my heart
I couldn't fight
Or make a blast
Thinking the cat will bite
Spitting like a dart
Unclimbable height
Had to fly with a kite
Like the horse and the knight
Doing what I thought is right
My fears brings out many fart
The cat had to give a rant
Though I hate rat and bat
Not even in the art
They all leave me to pant
Till I had nothing to act
All I could do was to shout

Mobile; 08169429926,08168103639
Email; deeyoke@gmail.com,
oladayookelola@yahoo.com
Blog; http://www.okelolaoladayo.blogspot.com
Facebook; okelola oladayo joseph(Aare)
Twitter; @ deeyoke

www.ingramcontent.com/pod-product-compliance
Lightning Source LLC
Chambersburg PA
CBHW032027040426
42448CB00006B/741